BEYOND
DISAPPOINTMENT
HOPE

BEYOND DISAPPOINTMENT
HOPE

PHILLIP R. STOUT

Beacon Hill Press of Kansas City
Kansas City, Mo.

Dedicated to my father-in-law,
Rev. Warren Posey,
who displayed great faith
and character in the face of
devastating disappointment

Contents

Foreword

All of us deal with disappointments—either with ourselves, others, or, yes, even God. How do we deal with such disappointments? We all need help along these lines. Here is a book that addresses disappointments, and does it well. There is realism in the writing, and a depth of truth that gives handles for the journey through the disappointing times.

Disappointments sometimes come in bunches. They are real, frustrating, and, well, disappointing. We need somewhere to turn and Someone who can finally bring meaning and recovery to the disappointed heart. This book offers hope, for it anchors its resources, ultimately, in Christ.

Pastor Stout is tuned into the daily lives of people. He walks with people through their hurting moments. He cares about what people face and, in this book, brings God's Word to bear precious answers and help for all rebounding from disappointment.

Here is a book that speaks to needs—needs like you and I have. The real ones, the nitty-gritty, gut-wrenching kind. But this is not a "get more faith and get on with it" book. Rather, it is a walk along the reality lane, acknowledging that disappointment can shatter an individual and leave the heart scattered with the debris of doubt and disillusionment. Where to go with the debris of disappointment is what this book is about. It is a map out of the lowlands to trust, healing, and understanding.

I am pleased to encourage you to read this book. It is for everyone. For somewhere along the journey, sometimes out of nowhere, disappointment pays a visit. It comes with jolting numbness and scary reality. This book will help the one going through a disappointing experience, or, it will prepare you for the next one.

As you read, may you sense this book as a tool leading you to Christ, and to His comfort and love.

—C. Neil Strait, *District Superintendent*
Michigan District, Church of the Nazarene

Acknowledgments

It is a privilege to acknowledge three wonderful friends who are responsible for making this book a reality. First of all I want to thank my mentor and friend, Dr. C. Neil Strait. It was he who encouraged me to write this book and then encouraged me along the way. When he first asked me to consider writing it, I asked if he would keep me accountable to complete the task. He certainly did. (I wish I had a nickel for every time he asked me when chapter 1 would be finished.)

Second, I would like to thank my good friend and co-worker, Hilda McCollum. Not only do I thank her for the hours she spent at the word processor, but also I deeply appreciate the enthusiasm she brought to the project.

Finally, I want to acknowledge my best friend and wife, Carol. Her evaluations and suggestions help me communicate. Her encouragement is priceless.

Without these three people this book would never have been written. They believed in what I had to say, and they believe in me. I wish everyone had friends like them.

Introduction

It was the looks on their faces I will remember the most. During the Easter specials at our church, I announced I would preach a series of sermons the next month titled "Dealing with Life's Disappointments." Several members of my congregation said they were looking forward to the series, and attendance was high.

But the thing I will never forget were the looks on their faces that month. There was a crippled woman slipping into the back pew during the early service. There was the wife of a paraplegic, sitting on the third row and hanging on every word. There were people experiencing troubled marriages, wiping tears from their eyes, and adults who had been victimized in childhood weeping as I spoke of disappointment inflicted by others.

This experience taught me what I was trying to teach. We have all experienced bitter disappointment.

Some people think they have a corner on disappointment. They believe no one has suffered like they have. This book is for them.

Some people think their suffering is insignificant. They were never abused as children. They never felt the pain of a failed marriage. Yet, there is deep disappointment with the way they have managed their own lives. And there is unspoken disappointment with the God who allowed them to be less than they could be and should be. This book is for them.

Some have used their disappointment as an excuse to throw in the towel. No, they haven't taken their lives; they've just quit living their lives. This book is for them.

Some want to rise above the disappointments of the past. More than just coping with disappointments, they want to be victorious in spite of them. They want to use them as steps to a higher level of living and a closer walk with Jesus Christ. The fact you are reading these words probably places you in that category. This book is for you.

Whether you have been disappointed with yourself, disappointed with others, disappointed with the church, or disappointed with God, you are not alone. You have been preceded by survivors and thrivers. They did not make it by denying their disappointment. They did not make it by pretending. They were victorious by being honest with themselves, honest with others, and honest with God. And beyond disappointment they discovered hope.

·1·

Disappointment with Yourself

When we talk about the disappointments of life we soon realize we all stand on common ground. Every one of us has experienced disappointments; at times, bitter disappointments.

One of the fascinating things that happens to me as a pastor is many people come to me and say, "Pastor, I'm different from anyone else in your congregation." Then they tell me about their disappointments. They tell me about the disappointments others have heaped on them. Then they center in on the way they've disappointed themselves through their past sins and their past failures. They usually sum it up by saying, "I know there's no one else like me in your congregation. Would I be welcome in your church?" I always want to say, "Stick around because tomorrow there's someone just like you who's going to come and see me." All of us have failed miserably in our lives. All of us have disappointed ourselves.

One of the ways the enemy wants to isolate you is to tell you you're on your own. No one has fouled up as badly as you have. When the enemy convinces you of that lie, he helps you build a wall around yourself, a wall of loneliness. You begin to close in on yourself. And soon you are overwhelmed because alone you cannot deal with the disappointments you've heaped on yourself.

So right up front I want to tell you you're among friends. You're among people who have one thing in common with you; we've all disappointed ourselves bitterly.

What Is Disappointment?

What is disappointment? Where does it come from? Disappointment is simply the result of unfulfilled expectations. It occurs when "our expectations exceed our experience."[1] It is the negative that follows the positive. Anticipation, expectation, and hope can be positive and highly exhilarating experiences. Disappointment is that crushing blow that mocks all our dreams. It says, "I told you so! You should never have hoped, never have dreamed."

Because disappointment results from unfulfilled expectations, it follows that the greater the expectation, the greater the potential for disappointment. If I went to a bad concert, I would leave the concert saying, "I wasted an evening on a lousy concert. No big deal." But if I had anticipated the concert for three months, if people had told me the music group was fabulous, I would leave the concert saying, "What a disappointment."

Let's go one step farther. If I had spent big money on the concert tickets, made reservations at a premier restaurant, bought my wife a new dress, and rented a tuxedo, my expectation would be running pretty high. I would be expecting one of the greatest evenings I had experienced in a long time. If, that evening, the car wouldn't start and we never left the driveway, it would be a disappointment I would remember for years. Why? Because I invested so much. I invested money, time, and most of all, hope and expectation.

The greater the investment, the greater the expectation. The greater the expectation, the greater the potential for disappointment.

Deal with Disappointments

There's one easy, surefire way to avoid disappointment. Never expect anything. Some people live that way. Some people are so guarded against disappointment they have promised themselves never to expect anything positive out of life.

I see it all the time. As the holiday season approaches, some people downplay the excitement of the season. They don't want to expect a joyful Christmas because they're afraid expectation will lead to disappointment. Perhaps they remember a painful Christmas from their childhood. Perhaps it was more recent. Christmas can be an incredibly painful time because it brings memories of dashed hopes and unfulfilled expectations.

I hear it all the time. "I don't want to get my hopes up." Sometimes it would be more honest to say, "*I'm afraid* to get my hopes up." I think of the couple who experienced a miscarriage and how frightening it was the second time a pregnancy occurred. They wanted to be expectant. They wanted to be joyful about a child, but they were afraid. "What if we're disappointed again?"

If we allow ourselves, we can go through life with our guard up, cutting off expectation to head off disappointment. The problem with that approach to life is that we choke off so much of our emotional energy. Part of the thrill of life comes from emotions of joy and emotions of expectation.

Tony Campolo calls this the "passionless generation." He says there's no passion in the world anymore. There's no passion in church. There's no passion in marital relationships. He laments that people aren't passionate in their work or passionate in their play. He says people don't even know how to sin anymore because they can't do it with passion![2] Amazing.

If we say, "I'm not going to hope; I'm not going to expect," then we cut off so much of the life God has given us. Hope, expectation, and joy all go together. Therefore, our task is not to learn how to avoid disappointment. We must learn how to deal with disappointment.

Self-inflicted Disappointment

First of all, to deal with disappointment within ourselves, we must learn to forgive ourselves. I use the word "learn" because most of us don't know how to forgive ourselves.

How can we learn? I believe we learn self-forgiveness the same way we learn every spiritual lesson in life. We look to the Father. How do I learn to love? I look at how the Father loves. How do I learn to care? I look at how the Father cares. How do I learn to forgive? I look at how the Father forgives. Then I take the principles I've learned about forgiving and use them to forgive myself.

Forgiveness

To understand what forgiveness is, it may be helpful to understand what forgiveness is not. First, to forgive is not to overlook. Some people can't forgive themselves because they think to forgive is to simply overlook their sins, deny their sins, and forget their sins. Defining forgiveness in this manner makes it virtually impossible to forgive oneself. As hard as we try, we're not going to forget about those disappointments and failures in our lives. We're not going to put them out of our minds! We simply cannot overlook them.

In an attempt to forget their sins and disappointments of the past, some people get busier. Some try to cover up the failures with successes. They attempt to offset great disappointments with great accomplishments.

But that's not how God forgives. God does not forgive by overlooking our sin. He does not see our sin and say, "That's nothing. We'll just overlook it. It's no big deal." It is a big deal. My sins were such a big deal that He died on the Cross to forgive me of them. He didn't overlook them; He dealt with them. To forgive is not to overlook.

Second, to forgive is not to excuse. A lot of people think if they forgive themselves they're excusing all the things they did in the past. And because they regret their sins so much, they simply can't excuse them. They cannot forgive themselves because they will not make excuses for their past. They're afraid to forgive themselves. They are afraid if they do, they are diminishing the severity of their past sins. And deep down inside they are afraid if they diminish the severity of sin, they may fall into the same sins again.

That's why many people are afraid to talk about the love of God. Afraid to talk about the love of God? That's right. Afraid! They fear if love and forgiveness are emphasized too much, it will give license to sin. What a grotesque distortion of the love of God!

I recall one preacher I used to listen to on the radio. To be honest, I don't know why I listened to him. I guess I was just fascinated. It was like watching a street fight on the evening news. It's ugly, but you can't quit watching. I referred to him as "The Prophet of Doom" because he could never say anything positive about God. It was all damnation and the awesome, awful wrath of God—day in and day out. As I said, I'm not sure why I continued to listen, except that I was fascinated at how a person could live on a steady diet of that stuff.

One day I heard him say, "Today I'm going to talk about the love of God." I said to myself, "Wow. He heard about the love of God. I can't wait to hear him talk about it." I turned up the volume so that I would not miss the momentous occasion. He began by saying, "God loves us, BUT . . ." Then he went ripping down the same old road, talking about wrath, hell, and damnation. It was then that I realized that this brother was simply afraid to talk about the love of God. He was afraid that if he told us about love and forgiveness, we'd all go out and misbehave.

Where did we get this idea of forgiveness? Certainly not from Jesus. Jesus didn't forgive people and then say, "Go and destroy your life again." He didn't forgive them and say, "Now go live a wretched existence." Just the opposite! He forgave and said, "Go, and sin no more" (John 8:11, KJV). His forgiveness gives us the freedom to live our lives the way they were intended to be lived.

Some people cannot forgive themselves because they are afraid to make allowance or make excuse for what they know was wrong. This is not forgiveness. To forgive yourself is to affirm what you did was wrong. It is to say, "Yes, it was sin; it was bad; it was wrong. I make no excuse for it. But because of the grace of God and the sacrifice of Jesus Christ, I am forgiven. And I can learn from the Father how to forgive myself."

Third, to forgive ourselves is not to lower our expectations of ourselves. Perfectionists have a very difficult time forgiving themselves. They are so afraid if they make some allowance for being human, some allowance for their sin, they have lowered all their expectations in life. (This spills over into their treatment of others. For example, perfectionist parents are not very forgiving of their children's shortcomings. They fear that making allowances for failures of the past will invite failures in the future.) Again, this is a distortion of forgiveness.

I admire people with high expectations for themselves. If you have high expectations for yourself (as long as they are realistic), keep them. The great achievers in this world are people who have high expectations. But, you can cross the line when you become unforgiving of yourself and do not allow yourself to be a human being. That's not God's intention for us.

Again, how does God forgive? He forgives you and me, and it increases His expectations of what we can become. He forgives us, and it gives us the freedom to become what He wants us to be. He didn't lower anything when He forgave us. He didn't say, "I forgive you so that you can be mediocre." He forgave us so that we could be conformed to His image and filled with His Spirit.

His forgiveness was not a lowering of His expectations. Forgiving yourself is not lowering expectations for yourself.

Finally, forgiveness is not condemnation. Some people spend their lives trying to forgive themselves through condemnation. They punish themselves. They beat themselves up. They bludgeon themselves to death, not physically, but emotionally.

Some do it subconsciously by destroying the good things that come into their lives. If a relationship begins to go well, they do something to sabotage that relationship. Deep down inside they are saying to themselves, "I don't deserve anything good. I must pay for my sins." Some people punish themselves financially. Not knowing why, they will ruin themselves financially because they are trying to punish themselves for their past.

Forgiveness is not condemnation. Paul said, "There is now no condemnation for those who are in Christ Jesus" (Rom. 8:1). What is condemnation? It is damnation. It is destruction. And Paul is saying forgiveness cancels out destruction. Don't destroy yourself to find forgiveness or relief from the past. Don't sabotage your life.

When Jesus Christ forgives you, He takes all your guilt away. When He forgives you, He makes you right with the Father. Our problem is, we don't forgive ourselves.

I know people who have been forgiven by Jesus Christ. They are justified, cleansed, filled with His Spirit.

They are children of the King, and their names are written in the Book of Life. Yet they are not *experiencing* forgiveness. They are trying to pay for their sins and are missing the joy of having their sins forgiven. After God forgave them they never forgave themselves. That's an awful way to live. A Christian has to learn how to forgive like the Father forgave.

Isn't it amazing? We call ourselves obedient if we forgive another, but we consider ourselves weak if we forgive ourselves. We wouldn't dream of withholding forgiveness from someone else, yet we do it to ourselves all the time. As Christians we know we have to forgive. We are willing to be like the Father and forgive our brothers. But we will spend the rest of our lives destroying ourselves.

We will never deal with disappointment with ourselves until we learn to forgive ourselves.

To Do or to Be?

I know it is dangerous to read graffiti on bathroom walls. But I thought it would be safe in the men's room of the seminary library. It was there, in those hallowed halls of advanced theological and philosophical education, that I read these words:

Plato—"To be is to do."

Aristotle—"To do is to be."

Sinatra—"Do be do be do."

Well, it may sound like word games, but the fact is, we must distinguish between "doing" and "being." In fact, this may be the greatest single issue in dealing with disappointments you have inflicted upon yourself in the past.

Simply put, I can't change what I've done, but I can change who I am.

Jesus explained it this way:

The kingdom of heaven is like a landowner who went out early in the morning to hire men to work in his vineyard. He agreed to pay them a denarius for the day and sent them into his vineyard.

About the third hour he went out and saw others standing in the marketplace doing nothing. He told them, "You also go and work in my vineyard, and I will pay you whatever is right." So they went.

He went out again about the sixth hour and the ninth hour and did the same thing. About the eleventh hour he went out and found still others standing around. He asked them, "Why have you been standing here all day long doing nothing?"

"Because no one has hired us," they answered.

He said to them, "You also go and work in my vineyard."

When evening came, the owner of the vineyard said to his foreman, "Call the workers and pay them their wages, beginning with the last ones hired and going on to the first."

The workers who were hired about the eleventh hour came and each received a denarius. So when those came who were hired first, they expected to receive more. But each one of them also received a denarius (*Matt. 20:1-10*).

Doesn't this strike you as being totally unfair? After all, shouldn't the guy who worked all day be paid more than the man who was hired just one hour before quitting time?

It depends. It depends on how you measure a man. Do you measure him by what he does? Or do you measure him by who he is?

In this parable Jesus was measuring the hired men by who they were. Who were they? They were people who were called and chosen by the owner of the vineyard. They were "His men." Because He considered all of them to be "His," they were all rewarded equally.

It is a mistake to try to determine my worth by what I do. I must determine my worth by who I am. It is too late to change what I have done. But the good news is, it is never too late to change who I am.

Every one of us can look at the past with regrets. I will never forget a time in my life when I was presented with a tremendous opportunity for ministry. It was a weeklong event. It was a chance for me to touch many lives. Yet, because of neglect and preoccupation with other things, I didn't take advantage of the opportunity. I'll never forget when the realization hit me. I woke up on a Monday morning and sat on the edge of my bed and cried. I wept because an opportunity had gone by and I would never have the chance to retrieve it. I would have done anything to reach back and pull that opportunity into the present. I would have taken advantage of it the second time, but there would be no second opportunity. I'll never forget the feeling. I'll never forget the pain. It is the pain experienced when a person thinks about a failed marriage, a broken relationship, a missed opportunity, a terrible mistake.

You can think about something in your past and you say, "I'd do anything if I could reach back, grab it, pull it to the present, and fix it." But you can't. You cannot change what you have done. You cannot change what you haven't done. But you can change who you are.

Our society has it backward. They say you can't change who you are, it is chiseled into stone. They believe you can't change who you are, you can only change what you do. But that philosophy of life is full of regrets, frustrations, and disappointments. Every day of our lives we can look back and see we should have done something differently. We should have done something we didn't do. We shouldn't have done something we did. Every week of our lives we can look back and say, "If I had it to do over, I would do some things differently."

The parable of the landowner teaches us that *God doesn't pay an hourly wage.* In other words, my standing with Him is not based on performance. If it were, I would not be able to deal with disappointment with myself. My standing with Him is based on my acceptance of His invitation to come into the vineyard. I can change my status (even at the 11th hour); I can change who I am.

I can deal with disappointment with myself because although it is too late to change what I've done, it is never too late to change who I am.

·2·

Disappointment with Others

Since disappointment is the result of unfulfilled expectation, it follows that the higher the expectations, the greater the potential for disappointment. The deepest disappointments we experience in life are the disappointments we find in the context of relationships. It only makes sense. Our greatest expectations are found in relationships, so our greatest disappointments are found in relationships.

I may purchase a new car and expect it to be the greatest vehicle I have ever owned. If it turns out to be a lemon, I'm disappointed. But it doesn't change my life. On the other hand, if I enter a relationship (such as marriage) with high expectations and that relationship turns out to be a lemon, it will be a disappointment that follows me the rest of my life.

Let's narrow our focus even more. The greater the potential for intimacy in a relationship, the greater the potential for disappointment.[1] In other words, the people who are closest to you are the ones who have the most potential to hurt you and disappoint you.

I have a relationship with the girl who gives me my sausage biscuit every Monday morning. It's a pretty simple relationship. I go to the drive-through window at McDonald's and give her money, she gives me a breakfast sandwich, and I thank her. It's not a very intimate relationship. About all we have in common is some change and a sausage biscuit. There is not much potential for intimacy, and there shouldn't be. She may disappoint me next Monday. She may give me the wrong order. She may snap at me instead of giving me her customary smile. She may not be there. But that disappointment will not run very deep, because this relationship doesn't run very deep.

It is a much different story when it comes to my spouse, my children, my parents, my brother, my sisters, my in-laws, and my close friends. Those relationships hold great potential for love and intimacy; they also hold great potential for disappointment.

Our Expectations of Those Around Us

To deal with the disappointment inflicted on us by others, we must look at ourselves. The first thing we must come to grips with is our expectations of others. Sometimes our expectations of the people around us are unrealistic. Because our expectations are wrong, we are destined to be disappointed.

Now, don't hear me wrong. I am not saying that we should have low expectations of the people we love. We should have high expectations of one another. If we have high expectations of those around us and we communicate those expectations in positive, loving ways, we motivate our loved ones and help them bring out the best in themselves.

Dr. John Maxwell is a great mentor of leaders. He teaches leaders to have high expectations of those they lead, and he shares a simple story to illustrate how it is done in a positive way. Dr. Maxwell used to work for the evangelism department of his denomination. One of his tasks was recruitment of lay leaders. He traveled to churches, preached on the joy and challenge of lay ministry, and then asked for commitments to ministry.

At each church, before the service, John asked the pastor how many he thought would respond in commitment. Most pastors took a quick mental trip through the Rolodex, looked over the names of their congregation, and came up with an approximate number. John always promised a higher number and every time the pastor would be amazed at the number of people in his congregation who committed to the most exciting journey of their lives.

Of course, the pastor confronted John after the service saying, "How did you know so many would respond?" John had a simple, profound answer. He'd say, "I put 10s on all their heads." After a perplexed look from the pastor, John would explain. "You categorize your people. You say, 'He's a 7. She's a 4. She's a 9. He's a 2.' You have expectations of them based on the labels you have put on them. I don't know your people, so when I spoke to them, I spoke to them as if they were all 10s. I looked at them and they all had 10s on their heads. And they came through."[2]

The point Dr. Maxwell is making is high expectations, communicated in positive, loving ways, help bring the best out of people. So please do not settle for low expectations of the people you love.

Still, while you have high expectations, guard against unrealistic or wrong expectations. *Do not expect someone else to fulfill what is lacking in your life.* When I am counseling couples who are engaged to be married, I always deal with this potential pitfall in their relationship, this trap of unrealistic expectations. I look at the groom-to-be and I ask, "Are you happy?" He says, "Yes." Then I look at his fiancé and ask the same question, "Are you happy?" She says, "Yes." (They *always* say, "Yes." I guess if you are about to be married you are either happy or too chicken to admit you're not.) After we are done with this little game, I say, "Now you may or may not be happy and the fact that I asked has little to do with whether (or not) you are. But let me tell you this, if you are not happy, getting married is not going to make you happy!"

Some people are shocked by this statement. After all, that is why some people get married. They say they are getting married because they are in love. But many times it is because they are unhappy with their lives and they are expecting their future spouse to change that. They think that even though they have a negative, miserable outlook on life, if they find the right person, that person will make them happy. Those people are in for a terrible disappointment. Nobody can make up for what is lacking in another person's spirit.

A lot of marriages get into deep, deep trouble because one person is saying to the other, "Make me happy, make me happy." And as much as the other one tries, it is an impossible task. Over time, both become disillusioned. One is bitter because the other cannot make him or her happy. The other is burned out and wasted from trying. Some never learn this lesson. They jump from marriage to marriage, from relationship to relationship desperately trying to find someone who will make them happy. Marriage is unhealthy when we look to a spouse to supply what they cannot give.

Marriage is a beautiful gift from God. He ordained it. He takes joy in seeing His children receive joy in that relationship. When a child of God has found contentment and peace in his relationship with Jesus Christ, he is able to have a healthy marriage. If he joins with a woman who has found her source in Jesus Christ, their joy is increased. This is because what was lacking in their spirits is supplied by Jesus.

This, of course, is true in all of our relationships. We must not expect someone else to make up for what is lacking in our lives. Countless friendships have been destroyed because persons of low self-esteem expected their friends to give them self-worth. This brought about unspoken demands that were impossible to fulfill. And because the expectations were high, disappointment was deep.

I teach a seminar for teenagers titled "How to Raise Your Parents in These Troubled Times." Teenagers must learn the basics of raising parents. (It's a dirty job, but somebody has to do it.) As I try to teach them, I let them in on an ugly little secret. Most of them have figured it out already, but it helps to hear it verbalized. The fact is many parents are expecting their own unmet expectations to be fulfilled by their children. Often parents are wanting their teenagers to accomplish something they could not accomplish or be something they did not become.

It is important for parents to come to grips with their own disappointments. If they do not and they expect their children to make up for those disappointments, they only set themselves up to be disappointed with their children. If you are not happy, your children cannot make you happy.

Your spouse cannot make you happy. Your children cannot make you happy. Your friends cannot make you happy. Your pastor cannot make you happy. If you do not have joy and peace in your existence with Jesus Christ, don't expect someone else to supply them, because every time you will be sorely disappointed. Do not expect someone else to make up for what is lacking in your own life.

When I find love, joy, and peace in my relationship with Jesus Christ, I liberate the people around me. I don't burden them with a terrible load they cannot bear. The people around me should not be expected to do for me what I should do for me with the power and strength of the Holy Spirit. When I allow the Lord to do His work in me, I free those around me to love me in a healthy manner.

Forgiveness

The first thing I must do to deal with disappointments inflicted on me by others is to make sure I have fair, realistic, and healthy expectations of those around me. The second task comes on the heels of the first. I must learn to forgive.

In chapter 1 I spoke about learning to forgive ourselves. I used the word "learn" because it does not happen naturally or easily. While the decision to forgive myself may be an event, the living out of that decision becomes a process. The same is true when it comes to forgiving others. In obedience to Christ we make a decision to forgive. Yet, it is a process for us to take this act of our will and, with the power of the Holy Spirit, translate it into spiritual reality.

Much has been said and written about coming to grips with the abuses heaped on us in the past. I am very appreciative of all the work in the field of psychology that has helped people of my generation learn to deal with the traumas of childhood abuse. Yet with all the progress, something is missing. As we have sought psychological and emotional healing, we have neglected the spiritual healing that must take place.

A friend recently came to my office so that together we could pray for his spiritual healing. He shared with me that he had been in therapy for several years. He said, "Phil, I think it has pleased God that I have been in counseling. It is the right thing to do. But I know I will never receive total healing if I do not ask for a spiritual restoration from God."

My friend was right. And what is true about our emotional healing is also true about forgiveness. Many of us have tried to forgive on a psychological or emotional level without forgiving on a spiritual level. Both are necessary. But spiritual forgiveness is impossible without the power of the Holy Spirit working in our lives.

I want to point out two powerful truths about forgiveness contained in the Word of God. Jesus' parable in Matthew 18 opens our understanding of forgiving others.

The kingdom of heaven is like a king who wanted to settle accounts with his servants. As he began the settlement, a man who owed him ten thousand talents was brought to him. Since he was not able to pay, the master ordered that he and his wife and his children and all that he had be sold to repay the debt.

The servant fell on his knees before him. "Be patient with me," he begged, "and I will pay back everything." The servant's master took pity on him, canceled the debt and let him go.

But when that servant went out, he found one of his fellow servants who owed him a hundred denarii. He grabbed him and began to choke him. "Pay back what you owe me!" he demanded.

His fellow servant fell to his knees and begged him, "Be patient with me, and I will pay you back."

But he refused. Instead, he went off and had the man thrown into prison until he could pay the debt. When the other servants saw what had happened, they were greatly distressed and went and told their master everything that had happened.

Then the master called the servant in. "You wicked servant," he said, "I canceled all that debt of yours because you begged me to. Shouldn't you have had mercy on your fellow servant just as I had on you?" In anger his master turned him over to the jailers . . . until he should pay back all he owed *(Matt. 18:23-34).*

What a fascinating story! A man owed a debt to his master that was impossible to repay. (In today's exchange 10 thousand talents would be millions of dollars.) He begged his master, promising to repay him knowing full well he could not. His master did not give him more time to pay his debts. He simply canceled them.

This servant was then given a beautiful opportunity. He left his master and encountered a fellow servant who owed him a few dollars. This was a very manageable debt. It could be repaid. The servant demanded payment to the point of imprisoning his fellow servant. He missed his opportunity.

The opportunity given him was the opportunity to be like his master. He could have canceled the debt of his fellow servant and it would have been said of him, "He's like the master." Simply put, *when I forgive I act like Jesus.*

Several years ago, as a guest speaker in a church, I dropped that concept into my message. I don't remember what I was speaking about, but I do remember saying, "When you forgive, you act like God." Following the service a man approached me with tears running down his face. He told me a story of betrayal. Ten years earlier he had been fired from his job. His best friend also happened to be his boss. One day he and his "best friend" were sitting on the porch, drinking lemonade and having wonderful fellowship. The next day he went to work and discovered his friend had stabbed him in the back, and he had lost his job. He never got that job back because of the lies his boss told about him.

He shared with me that he had confronted his friend and tried to talk it over with him. His friend would not even admit that he had done anything wrong. As a result, he did not forgive his friend. He said, "Phil, for 10 years this has been eating me. I've tried to forgive but just could not. Then tonight you said, 'When we forgive we act like God.' I forgave him." Then, as he wept some more, he told me that for the first time in 10 years he had peace. He spoke like a man who had just had a tremendous weight removed from his shoulders.

How could that have happened? How, after 10 years of trying, could a man forgive someone in the matter of a few seconds? It happened because the man experienced spiritual forgiveness. After 10 years of working on psychological and emotional forgiveness, he decided to be like the Master.

I am not saying that all emotional and psychological forgiveness is complete at the moment of spiritual forgiveness. As I said, it is a process. What I *am* saying is that emotional forgiveness is not enough. True healing is made possible when, with the power of the Holy Spirit, we become like the Master.

The second powerful truth about forgiveness can best be stated in the form of a question: *When forgiveness takes place, who is the beneficiary?* Sometimes there is more than one beneficiary. Sometimes the one who is forgiven benefits. There is always at least one beneficiary—the one who does the forgiving. The story of my friend who carried bitterness for 10 years attests to this truth. Jesus' parable about the unmerciful servant does as well. The man had an opportunity to be like the Master. The few dollars he had the opportunity to forgive were not that meaningful, but the opportunity was. If I take advantage of the opportunity to be like the Master, I am always the winner.

Some of the people you will spiritually forgive will never ask for that forgiveness. In fact, some of the people you will forgive will never even know they were forgiven. This is true of people who have had to forgive parents who are already deceased. If you consider forgiveness as only a favor you have bestowed on someone else, you may be slow to forgive that person who deserves no favor. But when you realize forgiveness is the liberation of your own soul, you will understand why God asks you to forgive every time, all the time. The forgiver is always the winner.

The "winning forgiver" is a truth that covers such a broad scope of life's disappointments. Even in the small disappointments of life, the forgiver is the winner. If we could learn that, it would change all our relationships.

One of the most disgusting things in life is to watch people hold grudges over the most meaningless, petty things. These people latch on to a misunderstood comment, an unintentional omission, or an unkept promise. Many times (perhaps most of the time) the person who has disappointed them is not even aware of the fact.

This happens all the time with pastors. As my church has grown, expanded, and changed, many have left. That is one of the prices of church growth and evangelism. Sometimes I will encounter someone who has left my church. When I see him or her I usually give a big smile and extend my hand. I have been amazed at the number of times my handshake has been rebuffed while the person even refused to make eye contact with me. With the people who are the most hostile to me, I sincerely do not know what I have done to hurt them. I am not suffering from their disdain for me. They are.

If you are holding a grudge against someone for a petty misunderstanding, I have one important question to ask you: How long do you want to be eaten up by bitterness? Is it worth it to hold a grudge for 6 months, 1 year, 5 years, 20 years?

I have determined my life is too short, my time is too precious, and my goals are too important for me to spend any time holding grudges. Bitterness is just too emotionally draining for me. I am not saying that small disappointments don't hurt. They do. When someone refuses to shake my hand and gives me a look of contempt, I hurt. I usually go home and cry for a few minutes. While I may hurt, I refuse to give any of my time to bitterness.

Keep in mind that we are talking about spiritual forgiveness. Even small disappointments will produce emotional pain. But Jesus Christ can give us power over bitterness. And His power is necessary for even the small disappointments.

But what about those deep, deep disappointments?

Dad and Mom are dedicated Christians who raised me, my brother, and my sisters with a rich spiritual heritage. My mother came to Christ as a child because a Sunday School teacher went up and down the streets looking for children to invite to Sunday School. This teacher found my mother, took her to church, and it changed her life. Mother eventually married a young Christian man and passed her faith on to several others, including her children and grandchildren. (God only knows how many generations will be impacted because a Sunday School teacher went to "seek the lost.")

Growing up, I did not know that Mom had been neglected and abused and abandoned. She protected us kids from it. My father's parents are godly people, so she made sure we knew them as our extended family. Over the years I began to realize more and more what had taken place in her life. Through my experiences in dealing with people as a pastor, I began to get some understanding of the psychological forgiveness she had to go through.

Several years ago, when I was just out of seminary, my grandfather (on my mother's side) passed away. In the process of his sickness and death, an amazing thing happened. My mother and father spent time witnessing to him about what Jesus Christ could do. They invited him to accept Christ. I believe that today my grandfather is in heaven because his daughter, the one he abandoned, opened heaven's doors for him. I preached his funeral. It taught me a lesson about a forgiveness that can go deeper than the deepest of disappointments.

A few years later my mother and I had the chance to talk about it. She explained to me that there was a psychological forgiveness that had to take place. This, of course, involves the process of bringing up those terrible memories and facing them head on. Most of the time this requires the help of a trained counselor. My mother, however, had to go through this alone because in her young adulthood there were very few professional therapists available. But my mother is extremely intelligent and is an avid reader. She dug it out for herself.

She explained to me that her relationship with her mother had never been and never would be like my relationship with her. She did not look to her parents for any kind of emotional support and would never feel close to them. Psychological healing does not necessarily bring estranged persons together. But there was a peace and freedom in her voice when she said to me, "Spiritually, I know I have forgiven." Those were not empty words, because it was precisely that spiritual forgiveness that God used to give her father the gift of eternal life.

I am not saying that forgiveness comes easy. I am trying to say just the opposite. In some cases I believe forgiveness is virtually impossible without the power of Christ's Spirit. The enemy will try to deceive us at this point. He wants us to believe we are bad or unspiritual because it is difficult to forgive. The difficulty simply means I must fall upon the mercy and grace of God who will help me be like the Master.

I offer a final word about disappointment with others. It is vitally important that we do not use disappointment as an excuse to be less than we can be. No one can dispute we are shaped by our past. And in many cases, we have been deprived or scarred by the past. Yet it is important that we take responsibility for our future. My circumstances and my emotional health (or lack of it) may not be my fault, but my future is my responsibility. If I need healing, I must seek it and not hide behind my past disappointments. If I need help, I must find it and not be irresponsible just because someone else was irresponsible.

Rising above the disappointment of others was incarnated in my friend, John. He went through the kind of disappointment that he never dreamed he would. His wife, who claimed to be walking with Christ, became involved in an adulterous affair with a man in John's church, who also claimed to be walking with Christ. These things shouldn't happen. We expect much more. The level of expectations that John had for his wife, his brother in the Lord, and his church made this a terrifyingly deep disappointment.

I will always remember those days together. John and I spent hours talking, praying, and crying. We don't see each other often, but those days bonded us for life. The thing I will remember most is the day John got that look in his eye. It was a look of defiance. He clinched his fist and said, "I will not give in to bitterness! I will not let this destroy me! I will grow closer to God than I have ever been in my life!" And that is exactly what happened.

Sometimes I tell my congregation, "It's Super Bowl Sunday." They usually look at me kind of funny, especially if I say this in April. They think I'm running a few months behind. But I explain that Super Bowl Sunday is the day when all the excuses are gone. Every football player dreams of playing in the Super Bowl. It comes at the end of the season when most players are pretty tired and almost all of them have some minor injury. But they would not dream of sitting out this game for a minor injury. They take the pain because they wouldn't miss this for the world.

But it goes further. They dream not only of playing in a Super Bowl but also of winning it. They want to go in the locker room after the game saying they were the best. Not one of them dreams of the thrill of making excuses after the game. There's no thrill in saying, "If my ankle had been stronger, I would have made that key block." There's no thrill in saying, "If my finger hadn't broken, I would have caught that last pass." There is no thrill in excuses.

I have to look at my life like it is Super Bowl Sunday. I want to come down to the end a winner. I don't want to say, "I would have been all out for Jesus, but someone disappointed me." There's no thrill in saying, "I wasn't a good father, but I have a good excuse. My father wasn't good." I want to put all excuses aside and play because I'm thrilled to be in this game. I want to endure any pain I have to endure in order to win. The disappointments of the past may not be my fault, but my future is my responsibility.

·3·

Disappointment with the Church

Everyone associated with the Church, the Body of Jesus Christ, has experienced some degree of disappointment. Remember, disappointment is the result of unfulfilled expectations. The higher the expectations rise, the deeper the disappointment. Also, the greater the potential for intimacy in relationships, the greater the potential for disappointment.

Except for our immediate families, there is no other institution or gathering of individuals in which we place higher expectations and in which we have greater potential for intimacy than in the Body of Christ. Therefore, the church is a place where there is tremendous potential for deep disappointment.

Church leaders are painfully aware of "The 1-11-55 Principle."[1] The 1-11-55 Principle states that on average everyone who is disgruntled with a local church shares it with 11 people. And each of these people share it with 5 more. So anytime someone is deeply disappointed by a church, there are between 50 and 60 people who take a low view of that church, most of whom have never even attended there. Some people make a career out of it. They're mad at six or seven churches they've never attended!

Now, many people have legitimate gripes with certain churches. Many times the church has been wrong and has inflicted pain. These disappointments are real, they are deep, and they take years of recovery. An example we have seen in recent years has been the handling of clerics who have molested children. Sometimes, through ignorance, these sins have been covered up by church officials. The result is that the victims feel raped, not just by a sick individual in a clerical collar, but by the church in which they had put their faith.

Some disappointment may not be placed in the category of child sexual abuse, but it is still very real. There is disappointment of being wrongfully judged; the disappointment of being misunderstood; the disappointment of not being able to use your gifts for ministry because the pastor is easily threatened by talented people; the disappointment of not feeling welcomed and loved by the body of believers.

Then, of course, there are those disappointments that are downright silly. I have heard of people leaving a church for reasons that I can barely comprehend. "The music was too loud." "The sanctuary was too cold." They did not get the public recognition they deserved. And on and on the list goes. And when people are looking for a reason to complain, a reason to justify their lack of support, they can always point to one of the pastor's weaknesses. He or she can easily be used as a scapegoat.

Let's face it. Pastors are people. They don't have more flaws than other people. They just have more opportunities to display those flaws. I remember when John F. Kennedy, Jr., failed the New York bar exam. People fail the bar exam every day. Many lawyers have to take it more than once. But because of young Kennedy's celebrity status and the scrutiny his family receives, his failure made the papers and newsmagazines. One headline read, "Many Have Failed, but None So Publicly." I immediately thought about my failures and those of my brothers and sisters in full-time ministry. We fail publicly. Many times I have left the platform after preaching with the feeling that I have failed miserably. I'm spiritual enough to know that God can use my weakest moments, but I'm human enough to want to run and hide because my failure was displayed for all to see.

Much of the disappointment people experience with the church is actually disappointment with the pastor, the most visible leader of that church. And again, this disappointment comes back to the issue of expectations.

One of the greatest, if not the greatest, source of stress for pastors is unrealistic and conflicting expectations. Unrealistic expectations often are placed on pastors by themselves as well as by other people. But what can be even more stressful are the conflicting expectations.

Most people want their pastor to be successful, but everyone defines success differently. Most people want their pastor to do a good job, but everyone has a different job description in mind. To complicate this issue, most of these expectations are not communicated, they are assumed. A person assumes that certain things must be accomplished by the pastor. The pastor is never told this because that person assumes that everyone would define the pastor's role in the same way. When the pastor, who may have a completely different concept of pastoral ministry, does not live up to that person's expectations, disappointment results. Because that person still assumes the pastor views ministry in the same way, the next assumption is that the pastor must be lazy, undisciplined, or uncaring.

Conflicting expectations become a mine field for many pastors. Every time a pastor chooses to live up to one person's expectations he or she is also choosing not to live up to another person's expectations, because those expectations are contradictory. Many pastors have left the ministry because of their disappointment over this very issue.

I have found that for a pastor to have peace and joy in ministry, he or she must make a decision that the ministry will not be driven by the expectations of those who sit in the pews. The vision and direction for a church must be given by God and then properly communicated to the congregation. Moses did not take a poll to see if Israel wanted to leave Egypt. Nehemiah did not ask if anyone thought it would be a good idea to rebuild the wall. God gave direction to these leaders who in turn gave direction to God's people.

I am not advocating dictatorial church leadership. I believe in shared leadership of a common vision. What I am saying is that the direction for a church must come to a leader in prayer and fasting. It must not come from a desire to fulfill the many conflicting expectations of a congregation. A pastor must be a consensus *maker* not a consensus *taker*. I believe most laypeople are yearning for this kind of strong, Spirit-led leadership.

Still, there will be disappointments in the pastor. I make it a habit to remind my congregation that I will disappoint them. I promise never to disappoint them through conduct that is immoral or unethical. I promise to walk as close to God as I can. But I also promise them that on many other issues I will disappoint them. I want my brothers and sisters in Christ to understand that it is all right to be disappointed in one another. It is part of living together in the community of faith. It is part of our growth in Christ.

Too many times people misunderstand their disappointment. They think something is terribly wrong with the church, the pastor, the ministry, themselves, or even their most closely held beliefs about God. What we must understand is most disappointment in the church is simply the result of uncommunicated, conflicting expectations. Disappointment does not necessarily mean that someone has lost faith or integrity.

The Nature of the Church

How do we deal with these inevitable disappointments? First of all, we must understand the nature of the church. The Church of Jesus Christ came into being at the intersection of the divine and the human. It happened in the second chapter of Acts in what is commonly referred to as the birth of the Church. The gift of the Holy Spirit was given to the followers of Jesus Christ. The Spirit of Jesus filled ordinary humans in a dramatic way. At that point the church came into existence. The word that Jesus and Paul used for the church was *ekklesia*.[2] It comes from the Greek prefix *ek* (out) and the verb *kaleo* (to call or summon). These ordinary people were called out to be human vessels carrying the Spirit of God.

People have always struggled with the concept of God being housed in human form. When Jesus preached in His hometown, they were amazed at the things He said. Matthew tells us "they took offense at him" because He was only "the carpenter's son" (Matt. 13:57, 55; see vv. 53-58). When the Spirit of Jesus Christ was poured into human beings on the Day of Pentecost, people chose to believe it was alcoholic spirits that had altered these people's behavior (Acts 2:13). We still struggle with many contradictions we perceive in the church because the church is a group of human beings filled with the Spirit of God.

I love coffee. In fact, I've become a coffee connoisseur of sorts. Because of this, my family and friends often give me gifts of gourmet coffee and coffee mugs. I have a collection of coffee mugs, but there are just a few I use on a regular basis. You can imagine what those mugs look like. They're the ones that are chipped around the top, have a couple of cracks in them, and have coffee stains on the inside. You may have similar looking mugs in your home. And the one you use the most is the one that looks the worst. It looks terrible, but you never throw it away. Why? Because it can still hold a pretty good cup of coffee. In fact, I've discovered if I buy Hawaiian macadamia coffee and grind it just right (not too fine) and put the proper amount in my coffee maker, a chipped, cracked, stained cup can hold a *perfect* cup of coffee.

A damaged container can still hold a treasure.

Paul writes, "God . . . made his light shine in our hearts to give us the light of the knowledge of the glory of God in the face of Christ" (2 Cor. 4:6). This description of the perfect gift is followed by a huge word that introduces the contradiction. The word BUT. "But we have this treasure in jars of clay."

To deal with the disappointments we encounter in the church, we must understand that God chose to place His perfection in chipped, cracked, stained people, "jars of clay." The hurts, the sins, the regrets of your past do not preclude you from being the dwelling place of God. The church is the mystical union of chipped, cracked, stained people who are filled with the Holy Spirit.

Paul goes on to say that this really is not a contradiction. God formed His Church in this way "to show that this all-surpassing power is from God and not from us" (2 Cor. 4:7). We are so eager to hide all of our imperfections because we fear they will disgrace the Father. The truth is that if we will be honest enough to confess our chipped, cracked, stained humanity, we will have the freedom to see God glorified in us.

I want God to use me and my church in great ways. My prayer is that God will do "immeasurably more than all we ask or imagine, according to his power that is at work within us" (Eph. 3:20). I want the ministry of my church to be so phenomenal that everyone can see it is God who is doing the work. I want people to look at us and say, "There is *no* way that those people could have possibly done that. It must be God!" In that way our imperfections will glorify Him because they will show "that this all-surpassing power is from God and not from us."

My Responsibility

The second step in dealing with church disappointments is separating the failures of others from my own responsibilities. Colorado pastor Doug Self says, "When I visit newcomers, I try to elicit the-church-did-this-to-me stories, because nearly everybody has one."[3] He goes on to say that he wants to empathize with nonchurch people who have been injured in their past dealings with the church. Because of their hurts, these people have neglected the church and God for long periods of time. The love and concern he shows helps them deal with the disappointment. Nonchurched, spiritually inexperienced, and spiritually immature people need this.

It is a real tragedy, however, when people inside the church use their disappointment as an excuse to be unfaithful to Jesus Christ. I am always astounded when I see people walk away from the Body of Christ after years of service and blessing. I understand that often people need to change churches. However, I am talking about the person who leaves a local church, does not find another church family, and over time (usually a short period of time) allows his or her relationship with Christ to deteriorate into nothingness. It is a strange logic that allows a person to say, "I have been disappointed by a human being, therefore I have no responsibility to God." Of course, logic has nothing to do with it. It is a lack of spiritual, emotional, and mental health that causes someone to destroy himself or herself spiritually because someone else did not live up to expectations.

It is equally important that I do not allow my disappointments to distract the church from its mission. Many of us have been socialized in a church culture that reinforced the "squeaky wheel." We were taught (by a multitude of examples) that if you are unhappy with something the church is doing, you should make enough noise or threats until it is changed to your liking. It goes something like this: "Pastor, if this doesn't change, I'm going to have to look for another church." The expected (and often received) response is: "Don't leave! We'll change everything!" You may think I exaggerate, but while this is not often the verbal response a pastor gives, it is very often the response that is put into practice. It is a fact that in many churches (small churches being the most vulnerable here), the entire mission of the church can be changed by one or two people willing to make enough noise until they get their way. This does not please God.

Jim Dethmer speaks to this issue when he describes various metaphors for the church. One metaphor is that of an army. When someone is injured on the battlefield, he says, that person is cared for. However, the general does not sound a retreat. He does not stop the battle to care for one wounded soldier. The general keeps pushing on for victory while someone else attends to the injured soldier until that soldier is again ready for battle.[4]

We will all be injured from time to time, many times as the result of disappointments. When we're hurt we have the desire to say, "Stop everything! I'm hurting!" We must fight that compulsion. We must do whatever we can to heal with the help of the Body of Christ. But we should not expect the church to stop moving forward. We must not seek to alter the mission of the church in order to heal our injuries.

This is a very difficult concept to understand, not intellectually, but emotionally. I have seen this struggle take place in the lives of many people. They have come to me with a complaint, confident that I would see it their way and make the appropriate changes in the structure of the church. When the changes were not made, they were confused. The rule book that had been scripted for them through past experiences said that a pastor's job was to please people—and they were not pleased. Some people can work through this with their pastor or other church leaders. Others leave the church and try to use that action as their final bargaining chip. They see it as "bringing out the big gun." They expect the pastor to come calling and at that time make a commitment to the changes they want. If a pastor does not respond, the person may become bitter. This can be avoided if we realize that our disappointments must not alter the God-given mission of the church. Again, it is a matter of separating our disappointments from our responsibility.

You See What You Look For

Dr. Elmer Towns is one of the world's foremost Sunday School growth authorities. He has identified what he calls "Ten of today's most innovative churches." These are some remarkable churches led by remarkable pastors. He calls them "pacesetters for the twenty-first century."[5] I was thrilled when I had the opportunity to send a lady to one of those churches. She lived in the community and would soon be moving to the city of this great church. I met her because she had come to me to express her deep disappointment with her pastor. She had been hurt by a man I know to be a very godly person. I counseled with her, helped her get involved in our congregation, and when it was time for her to move, encouraged her to attend one of the greatest churches in America. She did. And she was terribly disappointed.

This experience illustrates the fact that you can find disappointment anywhere. You can find it in a small church or a large church; a traditional church or a contemporary church; a church you call mediocre or a church that is recognized as one of the best. You can find it if you are looking for it.

If I were to ask you to find something beautiful in your yard, you could do it. Because you were looking for it, your mind would be inclined toward beauty. You might bring me a flower or a plant—or it might simply be a blade of grass in which you had found beauty for the very first time. No matter how well trimmed or shaggy your lawn is, you will be able to find beauty there.

The same would be true if I asked you to go in your yard and bring back some trash. When you're looking for trash, it is amazing how much you can find. I used to take a quick trip through the churchyard on Sunday mornings to pick up paper or rubbish that might have blown onto the lawn. I always intended to come back in with one or two pieces of paper in my hand, toss them in the wastebasket, and go about my other Sunday morning responsibilities. But without exception, I would find a lot of trash. I was always amazed at how many gum wrappers, broken sticks, paper cups, and bottles I would find. The lawn didn't look that bad when I went out. It was just that when I put my head down and looked for trash, I found plenty.

Now come inside my church with me. Again, you will find what you're looking for. If you are looking for flaws, you will find them. You can find them in the pastor, the music, and any one of our programs. If you are looking for sinners, you'll find them, because we welcome them with open arms. Also, if you look for the life-changing presence of the Holy Spirit, that is precisely what you will find.

I'm not saying you should be blind to the shortcomings and the changes that need to be made in the ministry of your local church. If we are to be truly what God wants us to be, we must be honest with ourselves concerning what is working and what is not, what is honoring God and what is not. I am saying that many times bitter disappointments with the church can be avoided when we open our eyes to see the beauty of Christ in the church, its leaders, its mission, and its people.

On any given Sunday morning, both kinds of seekers

enter the church. Those who are seeking out the shortcomings and flaws enter the church with an emotional white glove and run it over everyone and everything they see, hoping to find the dust. Those seeking help, healing, love, and the presence of God enter with anticipation.

Make a Decision

Stephen Covey talks about the difference between our "circle of concern" and our "circle of influence." Our circle of concern encompasses the many things we care about—our health, our families, taxes, the federal budget deficit, etc. When looking at all our concerns, "it becomes apparent that there are some things over which we have no real control and others we can do something about."[6] Those things we can do something about fall within our circle of influence.

When dealing with disappointment with the church, begin at the center of your circle of influence. I'm not talking about a group of friends or a circle of individuals. The center of your circle of influence is inside of you. Begin by influencing yourself. In other words, make a decision. The decision you can and must make is the decision to love the church.

By definition, the Church is the Body of Christ. I take that definition very seriously. In fact, I take it literally. Two thousand years ago God came to earth in the form of a man. Jesus Christ had a physical body like yours and mine, and He used that body with intentionality. His arms embraced. His hands brought healing. His tongue delivered the words of life. His eyes communicated compassion. And, finally, His blood ransomed Adam's race. After His resurrection from the grave, He stayed long enough to put His life and ministry in perspective for His disciples. Then He left with the promise that His Spirit would be coming to fill those very disciples. And the promise of the gift of His Spirit was fulfilled.

There was now a new breed of people on the face of the earth. Because they were filled with Jesus' Holy Spirit, their hands were His hands, their tongues were His tongue, their bodies were His body. That is why Paul said, "Now you are the body of Christ" (1 Cor. 12:27).

You must make a decision to love the church because the church is literally the Body of Christ. And how can you love Christ without loving His Body?

Several years ago while writing for a regional Christian magazine, I interviewed a local television news anchorman named Bob Hughes. Bob is a dynamic Christian who loves to talk about his faith. After I left the interview, I felt as though I had been to church because the Holy Spirit was so real in Bob's life. Bob came from a Christian denomination but found the Lord in a small fellowship group outside of his church. His faith was lived out in *both* contexts. This was disturbing to many of Bob's friends. Those inside his church wanted him to disassociate himself from those "fanatics," while his evangelical friends wanted him to leave his "apostate" church. Bob felt called to forsake neither.

I'll never forget the look in Bob's eyes as he leaned across the table. His words went something like this: "Phil, someday I'm going to stand before Jesus. When I do, I want to hear Him say, 'Thank you for strengthening My Body.' I don't want to see tears in His eyes and hear Him ask, 'Why did you claw, rip, and tear My Body apart?'" Those words made a lasting impression on me. At that point, I made a decision to love Jesus' Body.

You won't agree with everyone in the Body or everything that is done in the Body. Members of the Body will sorely disappoint you. But love is a decision, and you can decide to love the Body of Jesus Christ. That decision lies within your circle of influence.

My childhood, my adolescence, and my adult life have been lived in the church. I have been disappointed by clergy and laypeople. I have been disappointed by institutions within the church. I have seen godly people lose faith and lose their souls. I have seen the worst the church has to offer. But don't put the church down. That's very offensive to me because I love the church. It is my family.

Yes, I've seen the worst, but I've also seen the best. In the church I have met the most noble, courageous people that God ever created. In the church I have received unconditional love. I have been the recipient of the church's patience and understanding. In the church I have found leaders that I can respect and admire. It is my church, and I am astounded that God loved me enough to give me the privilege of being part of His Body.

· 4 ·

Disappointment with God

It has been debated for centuries. It has been used to defend God and to attack God. It has caused people to lose faith, and it has been a launching pad for people to exercise heroic faith. Although the problem has always been with us, it is new every day. Philip Yancey calls it "the theological kryptonite of our time."[1] It is commonly referred to as the problem of evil.

Simply stated, the problem is this paradox: "God is all powerful, all knowing, and all loving, yet evil exists in His world."

I remember when the problem of evil was an academic exercise. I found great challenge and excitement as I debated it in philosophy classes in seminary. It stretched my mind but was still relatively nonthreatening to my emotions. I recall a philosophy class in which the professor tried to illustrate to us that this was a life problem and not an academic problem.

Dr. Albert Truesdale was one of those professors who could really motivate me. I came into class ready to take his exam on the problem of evil. I had studied all the classical arguments and was ready to fill the blue examination booklet restating those arguments in philosophical and theological jargon. But Dr. Truesdale changed the "rules." I expected the exam question to read, "Explain the problem of evil and the various philosophical arguments (include their leading proponents) attempting to answer the problem. Critique each approach." But when I opened the exam I read: "You are the pastor of a church in a very small community. Two days ago a bus full of students was on its way to a high school football game. The bus plummeted off the roadway and every child was killed. You have been asked to write an article for the local newspaper on the goodness of God. Write that article." I understood then that the problem of evil was a life problem.

Later, I became a pastor and discovered that a large part of my life was ministering to people who had been blindsided by disaster. I learned the question would no longer be put to me in a seminary exam, but it would be asked of me face-to-face through tear-filled eyes. Also I learned I would put the question to God as I watched the suffering of family members and members of my extended family, the church.

Jim Dethmer frames the problem of evil. To help us understand the problem and the various approaches to it he uses the prayer we were taught as children: "God is great, God is good, and we thank Him for this food." He said the problem of evil could be stated this way: "God is great, God is good, and there's evil in the world."[2]

God's greatness and goodness coexisting with evil can still be an abstract concept for us. We say, "God is great, God is good, but there's war in Eastern Europe." "God is great, God is good, but there are homeless people in America." "God is great, God is good, but children are being sexually abused." Then after we are done with those intellectual puzzles for the day, we put them back on the shelf and go to sleep.

But suddenly we find ourselves in the middle of that puzzle. "God is great, God is good, but my father has cancer." "God is great, God is good, but my marriage is falling apart." "God is great, God is good, but my health is rapidly deteriorating." At this point, the equation changes. Now we are not only talking about the problem of evil but also talking about disappointment with God.

Remember, disappointment is the result of unfulfilled expectations. The higher the expectations rise, the greater the potential for disappointment. Our expectations of God are on the level of what we have been taught about Him. He is all powerful, so we expect Him to use that power to improve our lives. He is all loving, so we expect Him to use that love to keep us from all harm. We expect Him to be fair. We expect Him to intervene when He is asked to do so. Our highest expectations in life are reserved for the God of the universe, so when He doesn't come through for us, our disappointments are as low as our expectations were high.

Four Approaches

How do we deal with this deep disappointment? In his landmark book, *Disappointment with God*, Philip Yancey writes that all of us will not only experience this disappointment but also find some way to deal with it.[3] Some will apologize for God. Some will challenge God. Some will walk away from God. Every one of us will deal with our unfulfilled expectations of God in some way. Let's consider four approaches to the seemingly contradictory statement, "God is great, God is good, and there's evil in the world."

First, some people come to the conclusion that God simply does not exist.[4] The word "atheist" comes from the Greek prefix *a*, which negates (sometimes translated "not") and the Greek word for God, *theos*. Many people who cannot harmonize the evil they experience with the concept of a loving God find rest in believing that God simply is not.

This was the response of many survivors of Hitler's ethnic cleansing. As Yancey writes, some Jews "began with a strong faith in God, but saw it vaporize in the gas furnaces of the Holocaust."[5] Their expectations exceeded their experience, and their experience could not be denied. They saw the epitome of human depravity. They experienced Auschwitz, and the reality of the torture chambers could not be reconciled with their concept of a loving God. Therefore, many walked away from their belief in God. In the concentration camps, He was not real, but suffering was real. They did not come to atheism through their intellect, they came through their experience, which is a much more powerful force.

Forsaking belief in God is effective in dealing with disappointment with God. In essence the atheist says, "I no longer have any expectations of God, so He can no longer disappoint me."

A second way to deal with disappointment with God is to believe that God is not great, that He really does not have the power to solve the problem of evil.[6] This is the approach taken by Rabbi Harold Kushner in *When Bad Things Happen to Good People.* He wrote this book after watching his son die of a dreadful disease. According to Rabbi Kushner, "God is as frustrated, even outraged, by the unfairness on this planet as anyone else, but he lacks the power to change it."[7]

Believe it or not, this is very comforting for many people. It allows them to retain their belief in God and even retain their belief in a *loving* God. I was surprised to hear the comfort level in the voice of a friend as she embraced this theology. She said it made her feel good that God would not intervene in her life. At first I did not understand how this approach would bring joy or comfort. I discovered it simply fills the gap between her expectations of God and her experience with God.

A third approach says God is great but He is not good. He exists and He is powerful, but He does not care enough to participate in our lives. One of the ancient Greek philosophers referred to God as "the unmoved mover." He believed God is the powerful Creator, Mover, and Shaker of the universe, but God cannot be moved by the prayers of humankind. This approach says God does not love me enough to be moved by my pain.

This approach is similar to that of the deists who believe God created the world and left it to its own devices. Dethmer believes this kind of god is like the man who pulls the starter on a self-propelled lawn mower and then goes into the house and drinks lemonade while the mower runs through the yard wreaking havoc.[8]

"A fourth approach is to flatly deny the problem and insist the world is fair . . . the world does run according to fixed, regular laws: good people will prosper and evil ones will fail."[9] This is the song sung by many Christians today. They teach that if you have the proper amount of faith and ask in the right way, you will not have to deal with sickness or poverty. Yancey says, "I hear it virtually every time I watch religious television, where some evangelist promises perfect health and financial prosperity to anyone who asks for it in true faith."[10]

This denial can go even further. Some religions deny evil altogether. They believe evil is simply a perception problem on our part. What we perceive as evil is actually good.

Which approach do you take? Your first response to this question is probably, "None of those four! They're all absurd! I believe in God, I believe He is great, I believe He is good, and I don't deny evil exists."

This initial response may be true on an intellectual level. In terms of our statements of belief, all four solutions to the problem of evil are ludicrous. However, when we deal with disappointment with God we don't deal with it on an intellectual level; we deal with it on an experiential level. I believe born-again believers reject these as viable solutions to the problem but live one or more of them in their day-to-day existence.

To understand how I deal with the problem of evil, I must make the journey from my head to my heart, from my intellect to my experience. It is much the same as the way we treat an injured child. When my daughter, Bekah, was just a toddler, she fell and bumped her head. It was a pretty bad lump and looked as though she had received a mild concussion. How did I respond? Did I take her aside and explain the concept of gravity? Did I let her know that although she was hurting, gravity was actually a good force in our lives? Did I try to communicate that gravity was our friend? Of course not! Bekah did not have an intellectual problem, she had an experiential problem. So we held her tight and called the doctor.

When we feel disappointment with God, we are like an injured child. Sometimes we try to treat our experiential pain with philosophical rationale. Sometimes we say, "If I just knew why it happened, I could handle it." We make ourselves believe that if God, our pastor, or anyone else could explain it to us, the pain would go away. This is a fanciful response. Let's consider our experience. What approach do we take to disappointment with God?

Evangelical Christians do not want to deny the existence of God. So instead of walking away from belief in God, many Christians walk away from intimacy with God. They still believe He exists, but they minimize His existence in their lives. It is the same way we treat people who have disappointed us. We decide that we will not be disappointed by that person again. So we keep the offender at arm's length.

Our churches are full of people who, because of disappointment, are keeping God at arm's length. They never say He does not exist. But friendship, intimacy, and vital relationship with God no longer exist. Christianity has become little more than a religious exercise because the relationship is too threatening. There is too much fear that God might disappoint them once again. Like the atheist, this person says, "God cannot disappoint me again, because I no longer expect anything from Him."

There are Christians who through experience have come to believe God is not great. They would never say it with their mouths, but they no longer *depend* on the greatness of God. They prayed for healing, but it didn't come. They used seed faith, but still experienced financial ruin. They fasted and did all the right things, but God did not come through for them. Emotionally they say, "Never again!" They have rejected intercessory prayer as a viable force for their lives and the lives of those they love. They stand in church and sing "Great Is the Lord," but God's greatness has absolutely nothing to do with their daily existence.

Some Christians have emotionally adopted the third approach, and believe God is not good. Again, those words would *never* come out of their mouths, but in their spirits, the love of God does not exist. Many rationalize by saying they don't deserve God's love: "I had an abortion when I was young and God is punishing me" or "I had an affair several years ago and don't deserve to ask God to fix my marriage." The underlying assumption is God does not love me enough to intervene in my life for good. And at a deep level they believe, "I deserve to be punished by God." But, at an even deeper level they are saying, "No, I don't. God is not good."

Then there are a great many believers who take the fourth approach and simply live in denial. They will not let God or anyone else into their hurts because they are pretending those hurts don't exist. They believe a good Christian never doubts, never questions God. They can't deal with the contradiction between their expectations and their pain, so they deny that real evil exists. These believers usually take Rom. 8:28 ("all things work together for good," KJV) and make a quantum leap of emotional logic that says, "If all *things* work for good, then there is no evil at work in my life."[11]

I'm amazed at how dishonest we can be with God. Those who believe it is wrong to be honest with God should read Psalm 22:

> Why are you so far from saving me, so far from the words of my groaning? O my God, I cry out by day, but you do not answer . . . I am poured out like water . . . My heart has turned to wax; it has melted away within me. My strength is dried up . . . I can count all my bones; people stare and gloat over me *(vv. 1-2, 14-15, 17)*.

Those who believe it is wrong to share anger toward God should read Job's lament:

> If only my anguish could be weighed and all my misery be placed on the scales! It would surely outweigh the sand of the seas—no wonder my words have been impetuous. The arrows of the Almighty are in me, my spirit drinks in their poison; God's terrors are marshaled against me *(6:2-4)*.

Jesus verbalized despair on the Cross: "My God, my God, why have you forsaken me?" (Matt. 27:46).

We fear those kinds of words because we are afraid they somehow constitute a threat to God. Many times people say to me, "Pastor, I know I should not doubt God." I always tell them doubt is the beginning of faith.

People are afraid to ask questions. They say, "I know it's wrong to question God." Are we afraid we're going to stump Him? Are we afraid we're going to put Him on the defensive? Are we afraid He'll be threatened by our questions? I believe He is the One we should question because He is the One who has the answers.

People are sometimes afraid to express anger toward God. They live in constant denial of anger. I have talked with people who wallowed in guilt over the anger they were afraid to admit. I have pulled and pulled on them to finally say the words, "Yes! I'm mad at God!" Then I ask, "Have you ever been angry at someone else you loved: your spouse, your children, your friends?" At that point they begin to realize that anger with someone you love does not negate your love for that person. God is not afraid of your anger if you are willing to express it and allow Him into your anger. I am not saying that we should live at a level of despair and anger. I am saying that the starting point in the healing process is communicating our despair with the only One who can really impact the pain in our lives.

I am happy to say God is bigger than my doubts. He's not threatened by my questions. He's not angered by my confusion. And He does not turn His back on me when I am angry.

What Is Insurmountable?

Of the four solutions to disappointment with God, three are surmountable. If you've given up on the greatness of God, let me assure you God can deal with it. If you've given up on the goodness of God, again, He is bigger than that problem. If you are living in denial and are afraid to admit to fear, doubt, and disappointment, God will bring you along one step at a time.

One approach places you in a very precarious position: giving up on an intimate relationship with God. If you spend your days keeping God at arm's length, you also spend your energy keeping His power and wisdom at arm's length.

I remember listening to an ad about literacy. It said when you teach a child to read, you unlock the universe for the child. This ad concept caused me to consider what I believe about prayer. I believe that when we teach a person to pray we unlock eternity because we have given the person access to God.

Actually, access to God was given to us by Jesus himself. Scripture teaches about the most holy place, or what is sometimes called the holy of holies. It was the place inside the Temple where the ark of the covenant resided, the area that was known as the dwelling place of God. It was separated from the rest of the Temple by a curtain. This holy place was entered only once a year and then only by the high priest, who would go as a representative of God's people to atone for their sins. But one day, on a hill called Golgotha, the ultimate sacrifice was presented. That day the curtain in the Temple was torn in two from top to bottom so there was no longer any obstacle to the presence of God.

> Therefore, brothers, since we have confidence to enter the Most Holy Place by the blood of Jesus, by a new and living way opened for us through the curtain, that is, his body, and since we have a great priest over the house of God, let us draw near to God with a sincere heart in full assurance of faith, having our hearts sprinkled to cleanse us from a guilty conscience and having our bodies washed with pure water. Let us hold unswervingly to the hope we profess, for he who promised is faithful *(Heb. 10:19-23).*

Jesus has provided access to the Father. When we hold Him at arm's length, it is as if that access does not exist. We stand in front of the curtain as if we cannot pass through it, when in fact, it has been torn apart and stands open for us to enter. God has taken away all the obstacles between Him and us. But He will not force His way through the obstacles we set up.

It becomes a decision on our part. Will I allow myself to withdraw from the Father, or will I take advantage of the access that Jesus has provided to confront the Father with my hurts and disappointments? I cannot state it any better than did the writer to the Hebrews, "Let us then approach the throne of grace with confidence, so that we may receive mercy and find grace to help us in our time of need" (Heb. 4:16).

I vividly remember a time when I approached the throne of grace in a manner that was indeed bold. I wasn't looking for mercy or grace, I was just mad. I was vicariously experiencing disappointment as I watched a friend suffer.

Pete was a good friend who was part of our church's single adult group. Pete's father had abandoned him when he was a young boy, so he had been raised by his mother and grandmother. Now, at age 19, he was about to lose both of them. His mother was in the latter stages of cancer, and we all knew she would soon be gone. His grandmother was also ill. One day as Pete was wheeling his grandmother across the parking lot to the church, her wheelchair hit a stone and she fell out and broke her hip. I'll never forget the terror Pete showed as he ran into the church crying for help, "I killed my grandma! I killed my grandma!"

A couple days later, Pete and I went to see her in the hospital. She was a wonderful woman who would never say a cross word to her only grandson whom she dearly loved. But this day she was confused and disturbed because of the pain and medication. As we walked in, she moaned and groaned with pain and when her eyes fell on us she said to Pete, "How could you do this to me?" I felt knives going through his heart. As we walked out I said, "Pete, you understand what happened in there, don't you?" He said, "Yeah." I said, "Pete, it was the medication." He said, "Yeah." I said, "It was the pain." he said, "Yeah." In his head he understood, but in his heart he was dying.

At this point, I told God how to conduct His business. I prayed, "God, You can't let that woman die or Pete will think he killed his grandmother."

After several days, she went home from the hospital. Every day I reminded God of His obligation (as interpreted by me) to Pete. One night at ten o'clock the phone rang. Pete's mother was almost hysterical as she told me Pete's grandmother had just died. I hung up the phone, and I said to my wife, "How could God let this happen?" It was a 20-minute drive to Pete's house. I screamed at God and pounded on the steering wheel as I drove. "Was it too much?" I asked. "Was it too much to ask just this one thing? Pete thinks he killed his grandmother. How could You do that? Why couldn't You spare her life?" I told God how He had messed up, how He had done it wrong, how He owed Pete so much more. Through the whole process God did something wonderful. He heard me, put His arms around me, and together we cried for Pete.

Again, let me refer to the modern Christian classic. In *Disappointment with God,* Philip Yancey shares a story from a sermon by Frederick Buechner:

> It is a peculiarly 20th-century story, and it is almost too awful to tell: about a boy of 12 or 13 who, in a fit of crazy anger and depression, got hold of a gun somewhere and fired it at his father, who died not right away but soon afterward. When the authorities asked the boy why he had done it, he said that it was because he could not stand his father, because his father demanded too much of him, because he was always after him, because he hated his father. And then later on, after he had been placed in a house of detention somewhere, a guard was walking down the corridor late one night when he heard sounds from the boy's room, and he stopped to listen. The words that he heard the boy sobbing out in the dark were, "I want my father, I want my father."[12]

Yancey writes that modern society is like this teenager. "We have killed off our Father. Few thinkers or writers or movie makers or television producers take God seriously anymore . . . There are too many unanswered questions.

He has disappointed us once too often."[13] But, like the young man, we suffer as a consequence, ". . . sobs can still be heard, muffled cries of loss, such as those expressed in literature and film and almost all modern art."[14]

"The alternative to disappointment with God seems to be disappointment without God."[15]

Lazarus was very ill when his sisters, Mary and Martha, sent word to Jesus. The messenger implored the Master to come right away because of the severity of Lazarus' condition. Yet it was two days before Jesus even began the journey to Lazarus' home. Lazarus died. His sisters' grief was compounded by the devastating disappointment that Jesus did not care enough to change His schedule to come and help. Both Mary and Martha confronted Jesus, saying, "If you had been here, my brother would not have died" (John 11:21, 32).

On this side of the event, we have some understanding. The messenger said to Jesus, "Lord, the one you love is sick" (John 11:3). The word he used for love was *phileis,* which has to do with the kind of love two friends have for one another. A few verses later John says, "Jesus loved Martha and her sister and Lazarus. Yet when he heard that Lazarus was sick, he stayed where he was two more days" (11:5-6). The word John used for love was *agape,* which has to do with a love that only God can give. Yes, on this side of that event, we understand that Jesus allowed this tragedy because something spectacular was going to come out of it. We understand. Mary and Martha did not.

The fascinating thing about this passage is Jesus did not explain to Mary and Martha what He and the Father planned. He just cried with them. He hurt with them. When I hurt I don't need answers, I need Jesus.

The answer to disappointment with God is God.

·5·

Beyond Disappointment

I have stated repeatedly "as expectation rises so does the potential for disappointment." This may sound more like motivation to keep our expectations low. But in the arena of disappointment there is good news: the greater the suffering, the greater the potential for growth and strength.

If left unchecked, our desire to flee pain and suffering will go out of control. We fear it so much many of us have dedicated our lives to the avoidance of pain. Listen to our prayers. We pray for God to deliver us from financial problems, to alter a troubled relationship, to take us out of unattractive employment situations, to heal us. Again and again we ask Him to change the things around us. Many times the missing prayer is the one that says, "God, change me."

There is a fascinating and controversial passage found in the Book of Hebrews. Speaking about Jesus, the writer says, "Although he was a son, he learned obedience from what he suffered" (5:8). This verse raises a variety of questions about the humanity and divinity of Jesus Christ. While I may not be able to comprehend all the ramifications of this verse, I can understand what it says about suffering. Suffering was part of Jesus' development as He became all that the Father wanted Him to be.

If I do not understand and accept the fact that suffering can be beneficial to me, I will spend the rest of my life running from it. I agree with John Maxwell who writes, "The very things we want to avoid in life are the things that nurture us and shape us into the persons we should be."[1]

The person who constantly runs from pain believes happiness and joy are only possible apart from pain. They say they will be happy *"when . . . !"* "I will be happy when I'm out of debt." "I will be happy when I get a job." "I will be happy when my child gets out of trouble." "I will be happy when I have no physical pain." They live as though someday life will be free of suffering. The truth is, there are only a few small islands in our lives that are free from pain. When our current stress is over, another one will replace it. If we are postponing happiness for the day of stress-free, painless life, it will never come.

Suffering brings the *potential* for growth and strength, because growth is not automatic. We must choose to grow in our suffering and pain. This involves submission to the Father's will.

The prophet Jeremiah was directed by God to go to the potter's house where he would receive a message. There he saw the potter working at the wheel on a pot that was marred. Because of the flaws in it, "The potter formed it into another pot, shaping it as *seemed best to him*" (Jer. 18:4, emphasis added). As Jeremiah watched this scene, the question was raised by God, "Can I not do with you as this potter does?" (v. 6).

Today God wants to stretch you. He wants to change you. He wants you to be more than you are at this time. This stretching and molding is a painful process that tempts us to run back to our comfort zones, denying the Lord the freedom He needs to work in our lives.

We do not have a choice whether or not we will experience pain, but we do have a choice in allowing God to use it for our growth and strength. As Robert Clinton writes, "All leaders are constantly being trained by God, but not all of them learn from the training."[2]

To illustrate our spiritual "training," Paul seemed to enjoy the analogy of the athlete. Stephen Covey shares a story that, for me, brings Paul's athletic illustration to life.

I was in a gym one time with a friend of mine who has a Ph.D. in exercise physiology. He was focusing on building strength. He asked me to "spot" him while he did some bench presses and told me at a certain point he'd ask me to take the weight. "But don't take it until I tell you," he said firmly.

So I watched and waited and prepared to take the weight. The weight went up and down, up and down. And I could see it begin to get harder. But he kept going. He would start to push it up and I'd think, "There's no way he's going to make it." But he'd make it. Then he'd slowly bring it back down and start back up again. Up and down, up and down.

Finally, as I looked at his face, straining with the effort, his blood vessels practically jumping out of his skin, I thought, This is going to fall and collapse his chest. Maybe I should take the weight. Maybe he's lost control and he doesn't even know what he's doing. But he'd get it safely down. Then he'd start back up again. I couldn't believe it.

When he finally told me to take the weight, I said, "Why did you wait so long?"

"Almost all the benefit of the exercise comes at the very end, Stephen," he replied. "I'm trying to build strength. And that doesn't happen until the muscle fiber ruptures and the nerve fiber registers the pain. Then nature overcompensates and within 48 hours, the fiber is made stronger."[3]

My spiritual condition will depend, in large part, on my willingness to endure and learn from pain. Am I willing to have my spiritual muscle fibers stretched to the breaking point to grow strong in the faith?

As long as I can remember, I have had a burning desire to be used greatly by God. I have not always understood what that means, but the desire has been there. There was a time when I thought this desire was all that was needed. I believed God would take my desire and my availability and honor them with results for the Kingdom. Because this desire was alive at a young age, I expected God to give me "success" at a relatively young age.

Over the years God taught me many things about His call on my life. One of the most important concepts was capsulized by Robert Clinton. Clinton teaches that "ministry flows out of being."[4] Therefore, God's "approach is to work in you, and then through you."[5]

I have discovered there are no shortcuts. God needs to work *in* me before He can work *through* me. This takes time and involves many experiences. I must submit to His timetable and submit to the "integrity checks"[6] that will come into my life. This process is painful but necessary.

I must understand the love of the Father causes Him to spend my lifetime making me what He wants me to be. This understanding gives me patience. "If you know that God will be developing you over a lifetime, you'll most likely stay for the whole ride."[7] It also brings joy.

Paul was the one who most eloquently linked joy with suffering. He rejoiced in suffering not only because he understood that God was working in his life but also because he had a passion to be more like Christ. He viewed his suffering as a vehicle to fulfill that passion. Because Paul wanted more than anything to grow in the image of Christ, he could honestly say, "We . . . rejoice in our sufferings, because we know that suffering produces perseverance; perseverance, character; and character, hope" (Rom. 5:3-4).

That's the final word on suffering. Hope. Ultimately,

beyond suffering there is hope. Paul knew every disappointment that came into his life could be used by God to build perseverance and character. In fact, perseverance and character can never be built without suffering. And the character produced in Paul made him a man of hope. "And hope," says Paul, "does not disappoint us" (Rom. 5:5).

Notes

Chapter 1

1. Jim Dethmer, *Disappointment with God*, a three-part audiotape series produced by Seeds Tape Ministry, South Barrington, Ill., 1992.

2. Tony Campolo, "The Passionless Generation," *Youthworker*, Summer 1985, 16-17.

Chapter 2

1. Dethmer, *Disappointment with God.*

2. John C. Maxwell, from his teaching conference, "Everything Rises and Falls on Leadership."

Chapter 3

1. John C. Maxwell teaches this principle in his training conference, "Everything Rises and Falls on Leadership."

2. Jesus used the term in Matthew 16:18 and 18:17. *Ekklesia* is used several times throughout Acts, the Epistles, and Revelation.

3. Marshall Shelley, "The Many Faces of Assimilation—A Leadership Forum," *Leadership*, Fall 1990, 22.

4. Jim Dethmer, *Cause, Community, Corporation*, an audiotape that is part of the Pastor's Update Cassette Series produced by the Charles E. Fuller Institute of Evangelism and Church Growth, Pasadena, Calif., 1990.

5. Elmer Towns, *Ten of Today's Most Innovative Churches* (Ventura, Calif.: Regal Books, 1990), 10.

6. Stephen R. Covey, *The Seven Habits of Highly Effective People* (New York: Simon and Schuster, 1989), 81. Copyright © 1989 by Stephen R. Covey. Reprinted by permission of Simon & Schuster, Inc.

Chapter 4

1. Taken from the book *Disappointment with God* by Philip Yancey, p. 162. Copyright © 1988 by Philip Yancey. Used by permission of Zondervan Publishing House.

2. Dethmer, *Disappointment with God.*

3. Yancey, *Disappointment with God*, 179.

4. Ibid.

5. Ibid.

6. Ibid.

7. Ibid.

8. Dethmer, *Disappointment with God.*

9. Yancey, *Disappointment with God*, 180.

10. Ibid.

11. A better translation of Rom. 8:28 is found in the *New International Version.* I do not believe that all *things* work together for good, but I do believe "that in all things *God* works for the good of those who love him" (Rom. 8:28).

12. Frederick Buechner, *The Magnificent Defeat* (New York: HarperCollins Publishers, 1979), 65. Used by permission of HarperCollins Publishers.

13. Yancey, *Disappointment with God*, 253.

14. Ibid.

15. Ibid.

Chapter 5

1. John C. Maxwell, *Be All You Can Be!* (Wheaton: Victor Books, 1987), 125.

2. J. Robert Clinton, *The Making of a Leader* (Colorado Springs: NavPress, 1989), 90.

3. Covey, *The Seven Habits*, 290-91.

4. Clinton, *The Making of a Leader*, 46.

5. Ibid., 33.

6. Ibid., 58.

7. Ibid., 23.